BATMAN & ROBIN

BATMAN & ROBIN
MUST DIE!

BATMAN & ROBIN

BATMAN & ROBIN MUST DIE!

written by
grant morrison

art by
frazer irving
david finch
cameron stewart
chris burnham
batt
ryan winn

colored by
alex sinclair
peter steigerwald

lettered by
patrick brosseau
dave sharpe

cover art by
frank quitely

original series cover art by
frank quitely
frazer irving
ethan van sciver
david finch
scott williams
gene ha

batman created by **bob kane**

MIKE MARTS Editor - Original Series
JANELLE SIEGEL Assistant Editor - Original Series
SCOTT NYBAKKEN Editor
ROBBIN BROSTERMAN Design Director - Books
CURTIS KING JR. Publication Design

BOB HARRAS Senior VP - Editor-in-Chief, DC Comics

DIANE NELSON President
DAN DIDIO and **JIM LEE** Co-Publishers
GEOFF JOHNS Chief Creative Officer
JOHN ROOD Executive VP – Sales, Marketing & Business Development
AMY GENKINS Senior VP – Business & Legal Affairs
NAIRI GARDINER Senior VP – Finance
JEFF BOISON VP – Publishing Planning
MARK CHIARELLO VP – Art Direction & Design
JOHN CUNNINGHAM VP – Marketing
TERRI CUNNINGHAM VP – Editorial Administration
ALISON GILL Senior VP – Manufacturing & Operations
HANK KANALZ Senior VP – Vertigo & Integrated Publishing
JAY KOGAN VP – Business & Legal Affairs, Publishing
JACK MAHAN VP – Business Affairs, Talent
NICK NAPOLITANO VP – Manufacturing Administration
SUE POHJA VP – Book Sales
COURTNEY SIMMONS Senior VP – Publicity
BOB WAYNE Senior VP – Sales

Cover color by Alex Sinclair.

BATMAN AND ROBIN: BATMAN AND ROBIN MUST DIE!

DC Comics, 1700 Broadway, New York, NY 10019.
A Warner Bros. Entertainment Company.
Printed by RR Donnelley, Salem, VA. 8/2/13. Third Printing.
ISBN: 978-1-4012-3508-6

SUSTAINABLE
FORESTRY
INITIATIVE

Certified Chain of Custody
At Least 20% Certified Forest Content
www.sfiprogram.org
SFI-01042
APPLIES TO TEXT STOCK ONLY

Library of Congress Cataloging-in-Publication Data

Morrison, Grant.
 Batman and Robin : Batman and Robin must die! / Grant Morrison, Frazer Irving, David Finch.
  p. cm.
 "Originally published as Batman and Robin 13-16 and Batman: The Return 1."
 ISBN 978-1-4012-3508-6
 1. Graphic novels. I. Irving, Frazer. II. Finch, David, 1972- III. Title. IV. Title: Batman and Robin must die!
 PN6728.B36M67267 2012
 741.5'973—dc23
                              2012029955

CONTENTS

BATMAN AND ROBIN MUST DIE!

PART ONE: THE GARDEN OF DEATH 7
Cover art by Frank Quitely • Story and variant cover art by Frazer Irving
Cover colors by Alex Sinclair • Letters by Patrick Brosseau

PART TWO: THE TRIUMPH OF DEATH 33
Cover art by Frank Quitely • Story and variant cover art by Frazer Irving
Cover colors by Alex Sinclair • Letters by Patrick Brosseau

PART THREE: THE KNIGHT, DEATH AND THE DEVIL 59
Cover art by Frank Quitely • Story and variant cover art by Frazer Irving
Cover colors by Alex Sinclair • Letters by Patrick Brosseau

BLACK MASS 83
Cover art by Frank Quitely • Variant cover art by Ethan Van Sciver
Story art by Cameron Stewart (pages 85-99), Chris Burnham (pages 100-103, 107-109)
and Frazer Irving (pages 104-106, 110-116) • Story and cover colors by Alex Sinclair
Letters by Patrick Brosseau

BATMAN: THE RETURN

PLANET GOTHAM 117
Cover pencils by David Finch • Cover inks by Scott Williams • Variant cover art by Gene Ha
Story pencils by David Finch • Story inks by Batt (pages 119-129, 134-135, 138-140,
142-143, 145, 147-148) and Ryan Winn (pages 130-133, 136-137, 141, 144, 146)
Story and cover colors by Peter Steigerwald • Letters by Dave Sharpe

SKETCHBOOK by Grant Morrison, Frank Quitely, Frazer Irving and David Finch 149

BATMAN & ROBIN

BATMAN & ROBIN
MUST DIE!

LORD HAVE MERCY UPON US.

CHRIST HAVE MERCY UPON US.

HAS YOUR SON *BRUCE* REACTED AT ALL TO THE NEWS OF YOUR SHOCKING *RETURN*, DR. WAYNE?

WHEN DID YOUR MEMORY *COME BACK?*

WHO'S BURIED IN THOMAS WAYNE'S *GRAVE?*

PLEASE.

...DR. WAYNE JUST GOT HOME FROM A VERY *LONG,* VERY *ARDUOUS* JOURNEY TO FIND A CITY IN *CRISIS.*

EVERYBODY, *PLEASE.*

ALL OF YOUR QUESTIONS WILL BE ANSWERED *SHORTLY.*

RIGHT NOW, DR. WAYNE JUST WANTS TO GO *HOME.*

...*THE RETURN OF DOCTOR THOMAS WAYNE, A MAN PRESUMED DEAD...*

...*ONLY THE LATEST IN A SERIES OF SCANDALS AND REVELATIONS THAT HAVE ROCKED ONE OF GOTHAM'S OLDEST FAMILIES...*

WAYNE MANOR IS MINE.

GOTHAM CITY IS MINE.

AND SOON, WHEN THE BLACK SUN SHINES...

GNUHH

NO!

WHEN I GET OUT OF THIS, I'LL CRIPPLE YOU FOR LIFE!

...SOON I WILL BREAK AND CORRUPT THIS BOY YOU SO VALIANTLY REDEEMED.

BRUCE WAYNE FAILED TO STOP ME, MR. GRAYSON.

YOU DARE IMAGINE YOURSELF SUPERIOR TO A WAYNE?

YOU DON'T GET IT, DO YOU?

BRIEF BLOOM.

YOU'RE FINISHED.

THREE DAYS EARLIER.

WELL NOW.

HELLO AGAIN.

THIS IS HIM? HE DOESN'T *LOOK* LIKE MUCH...

ROBIN. PAY ATTENTION.

SO... YOU WERE *SAYING?*

...NO MATTER *HOW MANY* I KILLED, BATMAN, *MY* BATMAN WAS...*GONE.*

IT WAS AS IF SOMETHING JUST *WENT OUT* IN MY HEAD.

NO MORE *"CLOWN PRINCE",* NO MORE *"MEPHISTOPHELES OF MIRTH,"* OR *"MAN OF A THOUSAND FALSE FRONTS"...*

ONLY *THIS.*

SO I MEAN, *OBVIOUSLY* IF I WANTED TO GAIN YOUR *TRUST,* I HAD TO...TO *CONCEAL* MY IDENTITY AS *SEXTON.*

DISGUISE IS *ALSO* ONE OF MY MANY ACCOMPLISHMENTS, AFTER ALL.

DOMINOES.

FACT 1: INFORMALLY KNOWN AS *BONES.*

THE *BOX* THEY COME IN IS THE *BONEYARD.*

FACT 2: MASKED DETECTIVE *OBERON SEXTON* TURNS UP IN GOTHAM, ALLEGEDLY INVESTIGATING, OR MAYBE I SHOULD CALL IT *DRAWING ATTENTION* TO, CRIMES *YOU* COMMITTED.

SEXTON, *"THE GRAVEDIGGER."*

COINCIDENCE?

SEXTON, WHO CONVENIENTLY ARRIVED IN TIME TO POISON *MR. TOAD* AND SET UP *GABRIEL SANTO.*

A *BRANCHING* TRAIL.

IT'S THAT CRANKY, CREEPY ATTENTION TO *DETAIL* THAT GIVES YOU AWAY.

THROW IN THE DOUBLE MEANING OF "DOMINO," AS IN *ROBIN'S MASK*...

I KNOW YOU LIKE TO LEAVE *CLUES*, BUT I'M KIND OF *INSULTED* YOU MADE IT SO OBVIOUS.

JOKER, THIS IS *ME*.

I'VE BEEN DOING THIS FOR A *LONG* TIME.

I HAD *YOU* FIGURED OUT WHEN I WAS *TWELVE*.

SO WHO'S RIDING THE *MEXICAN TRAIN?*

ehhhehhh

BUT OBERON SEXTON IS A *REAL* WRITER.

HE HAD *BOOKS* PUBLISHED.

HIS *WIFE* WAS KILLED.

WE'VE BEEN CHECKING THAT OUT.

IN FACT, THAT'LL BE *THE KNIGHT* IN ENGLAND RIGHT NOW.

KNIGHT TO *DARK KNIGHT.*

LOOKS LIKE YOUR HUNCH WAS *RIGHT*, OLD BOY.

WE FOUND *SEXTON.*

HAHAHAHAHAHA

SANE?

IT WAS SEXTON WHO *KILLED* HIS WIFE, DID *YOU* GUESS *THAT?*

SO I BURIED HIM *ALIVE* WITH HER BODY.

THAT WAS *KARMA.* ONE *LAST GAG.* BUT THIS...

IF ONLY YOU COULD *TRUST* ME, JUST THIS *ONCE.*

I'M *TOO LATE* TO STOP THE *CHAIN REACTION* I STARTED WITH THAT FIRST LITTLE *DOMINO OF DEATH.*

AND NOW IT'S *ALL FALL DOWN* TIME.

EVERYTHING THE JOKER SAYS IS A LIE OR A TRICK OR A CLUE.

GESUNDHEIT, COMMISSIONER.

I'M SHARING THIS WITH *YOU* SO THAT WE CAN ALERT THE *EMERGENCY SERVICES* AND GET THE *MAYOR* ONSIDE.

FORGET OFFICIAL HELP.

THE MAYOR'S ALREADY UNDER *INVESTIGATION.*

THE... *OTHER* BATMAN CALLED ME "JIM"...

I'LL CALL YOU *COMMISSIONER GORDON,* SIR, IF THAT'S OKAY.

WE'RE *HERE.*

WELCOME TO THE *BAT-BUNKER.*

NO ONE CAN SEE OR HEAR US.

YOU HAVE YOUR OWN *SUBWAY STATION?*

OF *COURSE* YOU DO.

IT'S BEEN A LONG TIME SINCE GOTHAM CITY BELONGED TO ANYONE BUT THE *BATMAN,* RIGHT?

I LIKE TO THINK I'M JUST KEEPING THE COSTUME *WARM.*

BUT THE JOKER'S ONLY THE *BEGINNING* OF SOMETHING MUCH BIGGER.

I STILL HAVEN'T MADE ALL THE *CONNECTIONS.*

DON'T LET HIM UNDER YOUR SKIN.

DON'T LET HIM PLANT *DOUBTS* IN YOUR MIND.

IN THREE DAYS TIME, GOTHAM EXPERIENCES A *TOTAL SOLAR ECLIPSE.*

AN EVENT THAT'S SURE TO HAVE *SERIOUS* SYMBOLIC VALUE FOR THE KIND OF CRAZY PEOPLE WE'RE *DEALING* WITH...

BATMAN.

VOCAL I.D. ACCEPTED.

I KNOW YOU STEPPED INTO SOME *BIG* BLACK BOOTS YOU PROBABLY FELT WOULD *NEVER* FIT...

...BUT IF IT HELPS TO KNOW, MOST OF MY COPS *PREFER* YOU TO *HIM.*

IF HE'S TAUGHT ME *ANYTHING*, IT'S HOW TO RECOGNIZE A HIDDEN *PATTERN*.

I SAID OPEN THE DOOR, KID!

I KNOW ALL *ABOUT* YOUR REPUTATION.

LEOPARDS ARE LIKE DOMINOES.

THEY NEVER CHANGE THEIR *SPOTS*.

IT'S NOT THAT *FUNNY*.

A BULLET WENT THROUGH MY *JAW* AND CAME OUT OF MY *FOREHEAD*.

THEY CUT AND STITCHED THE MUSCLES, *BADLY* I HAVE TO SAY.

THE SMILE WON'T GO AWAY.

EVERYTHING'S A *JOKE*, NOTHING *MATTERS.*

I WONDER IF YOU FEEL THE SAME ABOUT THE BRILLIANT *MIND* YOU'RE ALWAYS SHOWING OFF.

THEY SAY YOU'RE *MAD*, BUT I SAY YOU'RE *NOT.*

HELP

SOMEBODY HELP

NAH.

SCREW 'IM.

I WANT THE *TRUTH.*

NOW.

SYSTEMS FAIL

CATASTROPHIC

SYSTEMS

...KRRKKZZ...
BLACKGATE...

BATMAN AND ROBIN
MUST DIE!
Part 2: The Triumph of Death

I'M NOT *LIKE* THE OTHERS.

I WAS RAISED BY *ASSASSINS* WHO TAUGHT ME HOW TO KILL *WITHOUT MERCY.*

IF YOU THINK FOR EVEN *ONE SECOND* THAT I WOULD *HESITATE* TO INFLICT SEVERE BRAIN DAMAGE...

WAIT.

...THE TRUTH...

...YOU SAID YOU WANTED THE TRUTH...

ANY TIME YOU'RE READY.

...THE *TRUTH* IS..

...THE TRUTH *IS*...

...I'M *USING* YOU...

I'M USING *ALL* OF YOU.

MY FIGHT'S WITH *HIM,* NOT YOU.

WITH THE *DOCTOR,* THE *BLACK GLOVE.*

...CUT ME... ...nnnaaa...

hkk.
NAH-HA
HA-HA

NNGHHHAHAHAHAHA

A *SMILING* ROBIN! A *LAUGHING* YOUNG *DAREDEVIL!* *THAT'S* THE WAY I *LIKE* IT!

A-HA!

I DIDN'T THINK YOU HAD THE POTENTIAL TO BE *FUNNY* AT *ALL* WHEN WE FIRST MET, BUT SOMETIMES EVEN AN *OLD PRO* CAN GET THE *WRONG* FIRST IMPRESSION.

A *ROBIN* WHO LETS ME MANIPULATE HIM INTO A *LOCKED ROOM* SITUATION?

A *ROBIN* WHO EVEN BRINGS HIS *OWN CROWBAR* TO THE PARTY?

YOU MIGHT BE THE *FUNNIEST* ONE YET.

...SELF-
DESTRUCT
UNLESS VOICE-
AUTHORIZED...

BATMAN!

YOU *HEAR*
THAT?!

BATMAN,
FOR GOD'S
SAKE, YOU
HAVE TO
GET UP!

WE'RE
SURROUNDED.

BATMAN!

SELF-
DESTRUCT UNLESS
VOICE-AUTHORIZED IN
15 SECONDS...

GNUH!

kka

...COMMISSIONER GORDON!

BATMAN! HERE! OVER HERE!

SELF-DESTRUCT UNLESS VOICE-AUTHORIZED

7 SECONDS...

DAY 2

FGNN!

...PAIN IS LIKE *FINE WINE* TO ME...

I'M *PERFECT.*

SO MUCH *MORE* THAN HUMAN.

PERFECTLY *CORRUPT*, PYG.

PERFECTLY *UGLY*.

YOU'LL MAKE A *WONDERFUL* LAWYER.

HOW CAN YOU SAY "UGLY" *NOW?*

BOTOX, DOCTOR.

ALL THE TOP *ACTRESSES* SQUIRT THE GERM UNDER THEIR SKIN AND HANDSOME MEN ON *TELEVISION*, TOO.

JE SUIS SHOWBIZ!

HNURRF

WELL, THIS IS YOUR BIG CHANCE TO *IMPRESS.*

YOUR AUDIENCE INCLUDES THE *MEDIA*, THE *MAYOR* AND THE *CREAM* OF GOTHAM'S UNDERWORLD ROYALTY.

THE THEATER IS *THIS* WAY, PROFESSOR.

YOUR *CO-STAR* SHOULD BE FULLY CONSCIOUS BY NOW...

MORE BOTOX?

NOT BOTOX.

NOT FOR *WORK.*

FOR WORK IS *PCP!*

I GIVE YOU GOTHAM! **THE NEW CAPITAL CITY OF CRIME!**

WHERE THE ONLY LAW IS THE LAW OF *MIGHT MAKES RIGHT!*

WHERE HUMAN LIVES ARE *COMMODITIES!*

WHERE EVEN MEN LIKE OUR STUBBORN, INCORRUPTIBLE *POLICE COMMISSIONER GORDON* MUST SUCCUMB TO THE *NEW ORDER OF THINGS.*

UNTIE ME! YOU'RE ALL UNDER ARREST!

HRUNT

THE RATS ATE THE YOUNG OF THE GOAT.

SOON YOU'LL DO *ANYTHING* FOR WHAT *WE* HAVE TO OFFER, GORDON.

YOU AND ALL THE OTHER INNOCENT VICTIMS OF PROFESSOR PYG'S *VIRAL NARCOTIC.*

INSTANT *JUNKIES.*

AS I HUNG ALL *DOWNSIDE UP* AT MOMMY'S BARBED WIRE BREAST, I *SAW* HOW TO MAKE THE *ULTIMATE DRUG,* YOU SEE.

IT SPREADS LIKE A 'FLU.

IT'S ADDICTION YOU *CATCH!*

A CRAVING THAT DESTROYS ALL REASON

ALL

KHE-HAH... SNUKK

IT'S THE JOKER!

NOT JOKER!

I SMELL BATMAN!

THAT'S THE MAN WHO HIT ME!

GET HIM!

HAHAHAHAHAHAHAHAHAHAHAHA

DOES IT *HURT* NOW?

I HAVE THE *ONLY THING* THAT CAN STOP THE PAIN RIGHT *HERE.*

BUT MY CUSTOMERS HAVE TO DO *EXACTLY* AS THEY'RE TOLD.

UGGNN

AAAAAAAAAA

BATMAN AND ROBIN
MUST DIE!
Part 3: The Knight,
Death and the Devil

AS RIOTING *CONTINUED*, GOTHAM WAS ALSO REELING TODAY AFTER THE RETURN OF *DOCTOR THOMAS WAYNE*, A MAN BELIEVED *MURDERED* DECADES AGO...

HOW DOES IT *FEEL* TO BE BACK HOME, DOCTOR WAYNE?

DOCTOR WAYNE! THIS WAY!

DOES YOUR *RETURN* HAVE ANYTHING TO DO WITH YOUR *SON'S* BIZARRE BEHAVIOR?

MY CLIENT WILL ISSUE A *STATEMENT* WHEN HE'S SETTLED AFTER HIS ORDEAL.

LOVELY COVERED IN DIRT, YES.

PENNYWORTH.

GOOD LORD.

YOU REMEMBER *ME*, OLD CHAP, DON'T YOU?

OH YES, SIR. I REMEMBER YOU WELL.

DAY 3

SECOND DAY OF CHAOS AS POLICE STRUGGLE TO CONTROL INFECTED RIOTERS IN MIDTOWN

DAY OF THE TOTAL SOLAR ECLIPSE OVERSHADOWED BY STREET VIOLENCE

REPORTS SUGGEST ALMOST 18% OF GOTHAM'S CITIZENS ARE ALREADY AFFECTED BY THE VIRUS THAT'S CAUSING AGONIZING WITHDRAWAL CRAVINGS

FEARS THAT THE CONDITION IS SPREADING WERE CONFIRMED

ORDINARY RULES OF BEHAVIOR ARE BREAKING DOWN AS PEOPLE SUCCUMB TO THE INFLUENCE

WITH STILL NO RESPONSE FROM **BRUCE WAYNE**, HIS FATHER **THOMAS** HAS APPEALED FOR CALM

IT SEEMS I MAY HAVE RETURNED **JUST IN TIME** TO PROTECT MY BELOVED CITY FROM **DISASTER**.

I'VE APPLIED ALL OF MY **MEDICAL EXPERTISE** TO THIS TERRIBLE SITUATION AND...WELL...

I DO BELIEVE I'VE FOUND A **SOLUTION** TO THE PROBLEM.

BUT WHAT I'M **PROPOSING** MAY NOT BE **EASY**.

I FEAR GOTHAM'S RECOVERY MAY COME AT A **PRICE**.

STOP POKING ME WITH THAT *GUN*.

I'M *NOT* A *PAWN* IN YOUR STUPID GAME...

I'M DOING THIS FOR *BATMAN*.

heheheh

IN THE HANDS OF A *GRANDMASTER*, THE *PRAWN* CAN BE THE MOST DANGEROUS PIECE ON THE *PLATE*.

NO FANCY MOVES, *HEAR*?

I'M THE MAN WITH THE MOVES 'ROUND HERE.

ASK *ALL* THE SEXY SKELETON GIRLS.

GIMME THAT *GEISHA HOBBLE*, YOU LITTLE FREAK.

LET ME LOOSE.

I EVER TELL YOU ABOUT MY PAL "BIG MIKE"?

GOD'S *TOP GUN*.

HIS *HEAD BANANA*.

WHAT ARE YOU *TALKING* ABOUT?

WHY CAN'T YOU JUST MAKE *SENSE*?

I'M MAKING *SENSE SQUARED*, SLOW KID.

THE *BANANA* REPRESENTS THE *PRIMAL GAG*, THE *FALL*.

I'M *WATCHING* THOSE HANDS...

GNNA!

I CAN CRUSH YOUR *WINDPIPE* BEFORE YOU GET A CHANCE TO SPEAK ANOTHER *WORD*.

OHHH, YOU NEED A *BAD OPERATION*, COMMISSIONER GORDON.

...NUMMM...

...PLEASE...

BUT AS I WAS SAYING, THE FACILITIES HERE ARE *EXCELLENT*.

THEY HAVE *DOCTOR HA-HA* AND *DOCTOR JOHNNY B. DAMNED*.

ALL THE *TOP* NAMES.

...*nnnrrgghh*...

DONE THIS TO ME.

YOU'LL ALL BE *BEAUTIFUL ONES* IN...

GRFF

MY *MASK!*

BASTARD!

SICK TWISTED!

GUTTT

I HAVE A BUNCH OF PYG'S ZOMBIES IN BACK!

COME *WITH* ME, KID.

YOU CAN'T HANDLE THIS ON YOUR *OWN.*

I HAVE TO.

BATMAN'S THERE.

GO!

THAT'S *HIM!*

THEY'RE ALL CRAWLING FROM THE BOX NOW!

YOU GET *HIM,* PIGGIE'S GOT *WORK* IN TOWN!

GNNN

GREAT. I KNEW I COULD COUNT ON *YOU*.

TOO MANY. I'M SORRY. I'M SORRY I DIDN'T LISTEN.

DON'T WORRY ABOUT IT. WE'LL *IMPROVISE*.

GNUHH

YOU DON'T GET IT, DO YOU? YOU'RE *FINISHED*. BRIEF BLOOM.

NNNAAAA

THE *.32 PELLET* WON'T *PENETRATE* HIS SKULL.

BUT IT *HAS* BEEN *EXPERTLY* PLACED TO FRACTURE THE SKULL AND CAUSE A *HEMATOMA.*

IN LESS THAN *TWELVE HOURS,* BLOOD ABSORBED INTO THE CEREBROSPINAL FLUID WILL RESULT IN *PERMANENT* NEUROLOGICAL DAMAGE.

OUR HANDSOME YOUNG ACROBAT WILL BECOME A *HUMAN VEGETABLE.*

UNABLE TO MOVE OR FEED OR *CHANGE* HIMSELF.

WITH ONLY BROKEN *MEMORIES* OF HOW IT FELT TO *SOAR...*

BUT I'M A *SURGEON.*

I HAVE THE FACILITIES HERE, IN MY *BATCAVE* BELOW, TO SAVE THIS WORTHLESS PIECE OF BIG TOP TRASH.

AND ALL I ASK...

...ROBIN, DON'T LISTEN...

ALL I ASK IS SOMETHING *SMALL* IN RETURN. SOMETHING *SOUL-SIZED.*

I DON'T *BELIEVE* IN SOULS.

THIS IS *MEANINGLESS.*

YOU'RE NOT THE DEVIL!

YOU'RE A MAN WHO *LIVED TOO LONG.*

WE *KNOW* WHO YOU ARE!

YOU SHOULDN'T HAVE COME BACK HERE!

NOT TODAY!

YOU'RE MAD!

YOUR DECISION CAN SAVE HIS LIFE.

BECOME *MY* CREATURE, SUBMIT ABSOLUTELY TO *MY* INSTRUCTION AND WHEN YOUR SOUL IS *EXTINGUISHED* IN MY SERVICE...

...PERHAPS YOU'LL FINALLY KNOW BY THE GAPING *HOLE* THAT *REMAINS* WHAT IT IS YOU'VE *LOST.*

THOMAS AND MARTHA.

THEY TOOK ME IN.

THEY SHOWED ME *KINDNESS.*

NOW I'VE TAKEN *HIS* FACE.

HE'LL BE REMEMBERED AS A *CRIMINAL,* SHE A *DRUG FIEND.*

THEIR SON *MENTALLY ILL.*

THE LEGACY OF *BATMAN* WILL BE ONE OF MONSTROUS FAILURE AND PERVERSION.

I WILL BE BATMAN IN MY GREAT *BLACK CAR,* PREYING ON THE *WEAK,* IN GOTHAM'S ENDLESS NIGHT.

AND YOU A VERY *DIFFERENT* KIND OF *ROBIN.*

WHAT *IS* THIS?

NEXT IN **BATMAN** AND **ROBIN**

BY MY *BLACKENED HAND* I SUMMON YE IN SEEK OF *KNOWLEDGE* OF THE *INNER WORLD,* MY DAEMON.

YE WHO KNOWS THE *WHERE* OF THE *MYSTERY BOX,* THE *ETERNITY SIGNS.*

THE *SECRET TREASURE* OF THE *MIAGANI.*

OMEGA ADAPTER

DARK SIDE

KNOWLEDGE

YES! *YES!* OMEGA ADEPTUS! *SIMON* FOR THE MAGUS NAMED.

SECRETS OF THE *GRAVE* AND THE *NIGHT.*

AND *LIFE EVER RE-BORNING* IN BLOOD.

THOSE OTHER MEN WERE NOVICE AND APPRENTICE AT THIS *INVERSE CRAFT* BUT NOT I.

HOW CAN A *REBEL* SUCH AS I FEAR *HELL,* THE NATURAL HOME OF REBELS?

TELL ME WHAT I MUST *DO.*

DRINK DEEP DARK TWIN

THE FOUL CUP

THE STARRY VENOM

FALLEN THING

WEAPON IN MY HAND

AURNTCH!

HHAURTCH

UNENDING

SHRRUPPT

MUH-MOMMY.

BUT HOW DID YOU *GET* HERE...I...I DIDN'T MEAN IT...

...SNURR...I TOOK A GUTLOAD OF LOVELY DRUGS...BUT NOW I FEEL ALL CREEPY...

FACED WITH A *CITY OF FILTHY JUNKIES* I'M MAKING *PERFECT LITTLE LADIES!*

EVERYONE *LOVES* ME BUT *YOU!*

QIIIORRLLIIU THE *CIRCUS OF SLUGS* IN THE *SPIRAL SINK* CALL ME THE *BEAUTIFUL ONE.*

PYG'S A BAD BOY.

BATMAN AND ROBIN WILL SSQZZZKKAK TO PUNISH YOU.

...I'LL PROVE WHAT THEY DID TO ME IN HOSPITAL...

...IN YOUR GOWN OF FLAME...HAVE PITY..WAIT...

YOU'RE NOT *MY* MOMMY!

GET ME SOME CLOTHES AND *DON'T* EVEN ASK!

THE MAYOR'S *DEAD* AND BATMAN'S ON HIS WAY TO *INTENSIVE!*

WE'RE TAKING BACK GOTHAM RIGHT NOW!

...*THOMAS WAYNE* WILL SAVE THE DAY, IF YOU ALL DO *EXACTLY* AS HE TELLS YOU.

THE *NIGHT DOCTOR* WITH HIS EXPERIMENTAL MIND CONTROL *THERAPY.*

THE *BAD DOCTOR.*

BARBATOS.

I LIVE TO BE YOUR WEAPON.

GIVE ME A *SIGN.*

QUARANTINE *LIFTED* AFTER THREE DAYS... MAYOR SURVIVES...

SO-CALLED *PROFESSOR PYG* TRANSFERRED TO *ARKHAM* MAXIMUM SECURITY VOWING *VENGEANCE* ON *BATMAN AND ROBIN*

CORRUPTION IN CITY HALL AND THE PLOT TO SMEAR THE *WAYNE*

YOU'RE *AWAKE.*

THE WORLD'S *TOP BRAIN SURGEON* PRONOUNCED ME *FIT FOR DUTY.*

IF YOU NEED *NIGHTWING* TO HELP YOU WRAP UP THIS CASE, I'M ABOUT READY TO GO BACK TO MY *OLD JOB* IN A WEEK OR TWO.

TWO *MONTHS* OFF, NO DEBATE.

THE JOKER SAID HE "DEALT WITH" HURT AND I'M INCLINED TO *BELIEVE* HIM THIS TIME.

BUT WE WON'T STOP *LOOKING.*

FATHER.

NEVER *MIND* ALL THAT... WHAT HAPPENS TO *US?*

NOW THAT *YOU'RE* BACK, WHAT HAPPENS TO *BATMAN AND ROBIN?*

WHAT DO *YOU* THINK?

BATMAN AND ROBIN WILL NEVER *DIE,* DAMIAN.

GET READY TO MEET THE PUBLIC.

...IN MY EFFORTS TO CLEAR THE NAMES [OF] MY *PARENTS,* I FOUND [M]YSELF CAUGHT UP IN AN [UN]LIKELY TALE OF *DOUBLE [I]DENTITIES,* IMPOSTORS AND CORRUPT CITY OFFICIALS.

I'M *SORRY* CIRCUMSTANCES COMPELLED ME TO ABANDON MY BELOVED CITY FOR *SO LONG.*

BUT I KNEW THAT *GOTHAM CITY* WAS IN SAFE HANDS.

SOME OF YOU MAY HAVE *WONDERED...* HOW DOES A MAN LIKE *BATMAN* AFFORD TO CONSTANTLY *UPDATE* HIS CRIME-FIGHTING TECHNOLOGY?

WHERE DOES HIS *MONEY* COME FROM?

WELL, THE [A]NSWER IS *ME.*

I'VE BEEN FINANCING BATMAN IN *SECRET* FOR YEARS.

MY *PARENTS* WERE *MURDERED* IN THE STREET RIGHT IN *FRONT* OF ME.

SO WHEN A MAN LIKE *BATMAN* APPEARED ON THE SCENE, WHAT ELSE COULD I DO?

NOW I WANT TO TAKE THAT COMMITMENT *FURTHER,* WITH *HIS* HELP AND WITH *YOURS...*

LADIES AND GENTLEMEN.

BATMAN'S *WAR AGAINST CRIME* GOES *GLOBAL* TONIGHT.

IT'S MY GREAT PLEASURE TO INTRODUCE WAYNE ENTERPRISES' *NEWEST* VENTURE...

Bats are common on the eastern seaboard of the United States of America, and those three that moon-minted night were no less conventional than the rest of their breed.

A little bigger, a little more aggressive perhaps, but otherwise unremarkable.

As insignificant in the great, great scheme of things as any other thing could **conceivably** be in any truly great scheme.

This particular bat, on that particular night, was just a common creature at the end of his forty-year lifespan.

With beating wings that felt weighed down by night-ages and moon-dirt, the old bat clambered into the dusk on its heroic, final flight.

It was a common creature, you'll recall, and its last desires were simple ones.

A safe cave to settle in.

A place to be alone.

A quiet perch to close its weary eyes.

These luxuries of a small, insignificant li...

But as our old bat searched for a cave to settle in, he was drawn instead to an odd, almost-familiar structure of stone and light and echoes with edges.

In it was the sweet sound of glory and order and architecture.

A new kind of cave.

It promised warm heaven of divine proportion.

A place where even the common could be accepted as sacred.

And in this cave there was a wealthy young mar...

His name was **Bruce Wayne** and he was bleeding to death, hopeless, with a bell in his hand.

A lost knight without a standard.

A soldier with a wounded heart.

A warrior without a **totem**.

A life without meaning.

PLANET GOTHAM

...WE'RE
AUTHORIZING
A MASSIVE CASH
INJECTION,
LUCIUS.

WE'RE INVESTING
IN BLEEDING EDGE
TECHNOLOGY AND
WORKING PROTOTYPES
TO SUPPORT BATMAN'S
WAR ON CRIME.

≶TT≷

MY *PLEASURE*,
MR. WAYNE.

THAT'S
WHY WE'RE
HERE.

IT'S GOOD
TO HAVE YOU
BACK TO YOUR
OLD SELF.

THESE ARE
THE *LATEST*
TEST DRIVE
MODELS.

MILITARY RECALL,
CONSIDERED TOO RISKY
FOR *DEPLOYMENT*, ALTHOUGH
THE MODIFICATIONS I MADE
TO THE *KEYPAD* SHOULD
IRON OUT ANY *BUGS*.

IT MAY TAKE
A LITTLE GETTING
USED TO...

HH

THE *G.I. ROBOT*
PROGRAM.
RECALLED AFTER THEY
RAN *ROGUE*.

I NEED A
THOUSAND BY
SPRING.

SOMETHING
TOLD ME YOU'D
SAY *SOMETHING*
LIKE THAT.

IT OCCURRED
TO ME THAT YOUR
FRIEND *BATMAN* MIGHT
BE *VERY* INTERESTED
IN THE POTENTIAL OF
REMOTE-CONTROLLED
SOLDIERS.

DEATH
WISHES

Behind the scenes of BATMAN AND ROBIN MUST DIE!
with Grant Morrison, Frank Quitely, Frazer Irving and David Finch

As regular readers of these collected editions will know, I sketch out pretty much all of the cover roughs for this series in my notebook at the start of the creative process. Here are the last of those scribbled ideas, alongside the polished, professional finished versions by Frank Quitely as well as the variant covers by Frazer Irving, Ethan Van Sciver and Gene Ha.

issue thirteen

Back in BATMAN #428, in 1988, the Joker had famously used a crowbar to beat Jason Todd, the unlucky second Robin, to within an inch of his life before blowing him away with a bomb. As is the way of comic book characters, Jason Todd eventually made it back from the dead many years later (and even made an appearance as the Red Hood in this very series), but I wanted to see the new Robin redress the balance in his own inimitable way—hence this image of a grinning, unrepentant Joker taking his skull fractures with a smile.

issue fourteen

I felt we'd missed out on the potential of an infernal cover depicting Doctor Hurt wearing Thomas Wayne's sinister, bat-like masquerade costume backlit by turbulent flames. The idea was finally used here, with the addition of a Batman who's had bullet holes blasted into his back in a domino-spot pattern.

issue fifteen

of the famous panel from DETECTIVE COMICS #38 published in 1940, where Batman solemnly inducts the young Robin into the crime-fighting fraternity.

Here the figures are flipped around, with left hands raised instead of right hands and a candelabra designed to hint at a trident or pitchfork shape, suggestive of the Devil. A huge, inverted cross appeared in the original drawing as an homage to the imagery of late '60s and early '70s "Devil" pictures such as *Rosemary's Baby*, *The Exorcist* and *The Omen*, but this was considered to be too "on-the-nose" and was dropped from the final version.

Mention must also be made of Frazer Irving's remarkably mental variant cover for this issue, surely one of the iconic Joker drawings of recent years.

issue sixteen

This was both mine and Frank Quitely's finale on the BATMAN AND ROBIN title, and the cover, like so many of the others, had been planned back at the beginning of the run and stayed fairly close to the original intention.

This was the first cover to feature our two Batmen—pinch-hitting Dick Grayson and the returned Bruce Wayne—together in action with Robin, and I'd imagined a kind of hierarchical "totem pole" stack of heroes with one above the other.

THE VILLAINS

The Joker

Wreathed in Satanic imagery, it seemed only right that the sinister Doctor Hurt should suffer Lucifer's fate and experience the Fall from Heaven one more time — here in its most farcical form. I decided that the Joker's elaborately constructed and telegraphed multi-leveled assault on Hurt would end with one of the most basic of all jokes — the ol' banana peel gag — but when I read up on the origins of the banana pratfall I was surprised and delighted to learn that a particular variety of banana, known as a Big Mike, was considered the most effective prop, due to its special slipperiness and a tendency to rot quickly to a frictionless mush.

St. Michael was of course God's head enforcer and it was he who cast Lucifer out of Heaven. Ah, serendipity!

See also St. Thomas and burial alive.

Professor Pyg

Like the Joker's elliptical, double-meaning dialogue, Professor Pyg's seemingly deranged rants are also stuffed with hidden allusions — in Pyg's case to a series of somewhat grotesque animal experiments that were conducted in the US at the mid-point of the 20th century and which inspired the self-styled Professor's horrific — and as yet unrevealed — origin story.

For those readers inclined to follow Pyg's schizophrenic snail trail to its grim source, the "Doctor Ha-Ha" that he refers to is both the Joker and behavioral scientist Harry Harlow, who conducted his infamous "wire mother/cloth mother" experiments on infant monkeys. "Doctor Johnny B. Damned," while it could as easily apply to Hurt, is also intended to suggest John B. Calhoun, whose Rockville barn rat population research makes fascinating (if uncomfortable) reading.

99 Fiends

With the exception of these characters, the villains in "Batman and Robin Must Die!" were returning faces: Doctor Hurt from "Batman R.I.P.," Professor Pyg from "Batman Reborn" and of course the perennial Joker.

The 99 Fiends were created as the enforcers for El Penitente (a.k.a. Doctor Hurt) and each was based on a different classical demon, with the majority of them deriving from the Goetia of the Lemegeton, a 17th century magical grimoire.

All 99 of the Fiends were carefully worked out, but in spite of my efforts I couldn't find a way to include them all on the page. Here, from the original script for BATMAN AND ROBIN #16, are a representative sample:

Glasyolabalas — a brutish man with a snarling dog on a leash and spiked collar.

Duke Agares is an older, wiry man with a crocodile skin coat and boots and a hawk on his arm.

President Buer is a big black guy with bows and arrows.

President Barbas has the lion as his totem and governs things mechanical, so maybe a little steampunk.

Duke Eligos, "a knight with a lance" — the homeless crustie demon version of Don Quixote.

Marquis Forneus is an outsize, hulking brute in green, with shaggy dyed-green hair and beard and filed teeth. The original demonic Forneus was described as a sea monster.

Duke Bune wears a necklace of three shrunken heads.

King Balam is a huge bear-like man wearing bear-like clothes, with double-pronged meat hooks that he grips in both fists and wields like Wolverine's claws. He and Forneus make a good pair of hulks.

Count Ronove is a big silent Native American bad man with a staff.

Marquis Leraje is a lithe, androgynous creature in green, with a bow and arrows like some evil Legolas.

Sir Furcas, Knight of Hell, is another evil older man, hunched and sneaking, with a pitchfork as his weapon.

Marquis Andrealphas has the style, colors, and perhaps feathers of a peacock and is roaring mad-eyed all the time.

Prince Sitri, a beautiful man; so beautiful, in fact, that it's creepy, otherworldly. His cheekbones a little too high, too refined; his lips a little too pursed, becoming almost proboscis-like; his eyes hooded, like some awful aesthete looking down his nose at us. White skin and a powdered wig, like Adam Ant's Prince Charming beginning a transformation into an insect. His skin from the neck up to his jaw line is tattooed with leopard-like spots.

President Caim carries a sword and has "blackbird" clothes, characteristics or logos.

Duke Murmur is vulturous in aspect.

Duke Gremory is a fit woman wielding dual swords and wearing a nun-like outfit and a cracked doll-face mask of beauty.

Following the supernatural, psycho-sci-fi of BATMAN: THE RETURN OF BRUCE WAYNE, which brought the original Caped Crusader back after over a year's absence, I wanted to change direction and tackle stories that were a little more international in scope, playing up the Bond-style gadgetry aspects of Batman's adventures. The high-tech Batman of THE RETURN, with his robots and jet-suits, was a nod in the direction of the future Batman from Alex Ross and Mark Waid's KINGDOM COME series.

I had no input in the cover art this time, leaving it to my collaborator David Finch to supply another of his iconic Batman images. Instead I sent David some thoughts on how we might revamp the details of the uniform and I include these below.

The Costume

As far as the Batman costume re-design goes, we need first of all to differentiate him from Dick Grayson — the current Batman — who will be continuing in his new role over in BATMAN AND ROBIN. Body shape comes into it — Bruce is generally depicted as more massive than the lithe and acrobatic Grayson, so the design can be constructed around his distinctive shape. It's easy to think the Batman costume is too "classic" to change much, but it's been tweaked on a feverish and consistent basis for 70 years, always retaining certain essential elements expressed through wildly different fabrics, decorations and drapery to achieve a fresh yet iconic look. Adam West's flimsy, hand-sewn nylon and George Clooney's outrageous disco armor are worlds apart visually and yet they are both clearly Batman.

With that in mind, here are a few thoughts to take into account or disregard:

General appearance

Today's audiences like a bit of authenticity, so the more "real" the costume looks — i.e., the more it seems like someone could actually put it together using the best available materials — the better. In *The Batman Handbook* Scott Beatty writes. "The costume is sewn from Nomex fabric, making it fireproof under even the hottest temperatures. More importantly the Batsuit is bulletproof, with Kevlar panels sewn into the shirt portion to protect Bruce's torso from ballistic projectiles, particularly in the area surrounding the bat-emblem." It also contains a mess of electronics, including a heating and cooling system and secure broadband communications.

Utility belt

I tend to favor a chunky belt as more "mythic," in the sense that it looks like the girdles worn by Greek demigods and heroes. And it's good to work out exactly what he carries in those pouches, pods or cartridges. *The Batman Encyclopedia* has various takes on the contents, as does *The Batman Handbook*.

Shield

Should we bring back some version of the yellow shield and leave Grayson with the simple black bat chest emblem? Although comics fans traditionally dislike the shield, it has the virtue of having been part of one of the biggest marketing campaigns in history. Tim Burton's *Batman* burned that image of the black on yellow shield (which looks like a gaping toothy maw if you reverse figure and ground) into the cultural memory of nations.

The shield is also used in the early animated series episodes, and Batman wears it throughout Neal Adams's groundbreaking run and for about half of Frank Miller's THE DARK KNIGHT RETURNS so there's more to it than just its ties to the "goofy" *Batman* TV show. I thought it could light up to project a bat-signal onto a crime scene or dazzle an enemy. It could even be powered down to black or gray so that it camouflages itself when necessary.

Just in case this sounds like I'm making a case for the shield, I'll happily go along with whatever looks best in the final design. Ideas welcome.

Cape & cowl

Looking through the various versions of Batman, including the Bruce Timm animated stuff, I've noticed that he always looks especially cool when there are no highlights on his cape and cowl. So how about we try making a feature of a matte black cape and cowl combo with no reflected light — a pure silhouette that dissolves completely into the background shadows.

Boots

The rugged treads of the Frank Miller and Jim Lee versions look more bad-ass so have a look at some current and concept athletic shoe soles and find something cool and up-to-date or a little bit futuristic.

Gauntlets

As long as they still have the three bat-blades, I'm fine with it. Again, keep them real by checking out the latest in racing driver gloves or firefighter gloves and see if there are some interesting new designs that could inspire a bit of detail and modernity.

Ears

Long or short? Horns or vanes? Your call.

Basically, I imagine the new international sex god Bruce Wayne Bat-colossus to be a kind of "definitive" distillation of everything we like into one hardcore, modernized and coolly understated package. Batman's look stripped of frills and brought back to its basic essentials. We're looking for a costume that's convincing, functional, sexy and modern. Something that takes him back to his primal roots and adds your 21st century cool comics aesthetic.

Easy for me to say! Over to you, Mr. F!

— **Grant Morrison**
Scotland
February 2011